DISCOVERING

GRACE

# DISCOVERING

# GRACE IN GRIEF

James L. Mayfield

UPPER
ROOM BOOKS
NASHVILLE

Cover Design: Cindy Helms
Cover Photograph:  Byron Jorjorian
First Printing: April 1994 (5)
Library of Congress Catalog Number: 93-6014
ISBN: 0-8358-0696-0


Printed in the United States of America

*A Special Thanks to Three Women*
*Whose Grace-Filled Living Helped Me*
*Discover Grace in My Grief:*

*My mother ~ Mrs. Kathryne Mayfield*
*My grandmother ~ Mrs. Knoxie Walker*
*My mother-in-law ~ Mrs. Betty Browning*

# Contents

ᵱᵱᵱᎶᵱᵱᵱ

# Preface

ᛒᛒᛒᛒ ᛒᛒᛒᛒ

This is a book written for persons who are in grief. It contains not only what I have to tell from my personal grief experiences but also what I have learned from other persons who have told me about their experience of grief and the grace they discovered (or that discovered them).

The goal of this book is to show some of the ways God's grace is at work in the various stages of our grief.

In order to have a book that is both practical and readable, I have used many illustrations. Each of these illustrations is true to life and rooted in actual experience. However, in order to protect the privacy of grief, I have modified all of the illustrations (except those related to my father's death) in order to hide the situations from which they came.

I publicly express my thanks to those persons who shared with me the grace they discovered in their grief: to Mrs. Myra McIlvain for her comments about writing style; to Dr. Thomas C. Oden and Dr. Ralph L. Underwood for their comments, questions, and encouragement; and to Rita, my wife, for her friendship, confidence, and conversation.

# ~1~

**Grace**
is the word I use
to point toward the
mysterious healing,
redeeming, reconciling
realities at work
in our lives.

# Introduction

ๆๆๆ๕๑ๆๆๆ

### A Road Map for Going Through This Book

Grief is a powerful and complex experience that happens to us when we have suffered a significant loss. Some form of death has happened. As a result, relationships are changed; hopes, dreams, and possibilities that were once alive are buried. An important part of our life is gone.

It takes time to adjust to significant losses. This book is aimed at this period of adjustment. It attempts to provide two types of information: (1) a description of this period of adjustment (sometimes called "the grief process") and (2) some insights from the heritage of Christian faith that I have found helpful.

The goals of this book are to describe the various stages of the grief experience and to point to some of the ways God's grace can be at work in each of these stages. It is hoped that by doing this, readers who are in grief will become more sensitive to the grace of God at work in their grief experiences.

Grief will be described in a series of stages or aspects. As each of these aspects of grief is described, we will explore ways God's grace can be at work. The stages or phases of grief identified in this book are: shock and relief (chapter 2), emotional upheaval (chapter 3), nostalgia (chapter 4), guilt feelings (chapter 5), physical reactions (chapter 6), loneliness (chapter 7), fears and doubts (chapter 8), anger (chapter 9), temptations to deny grief (chapter 10), and a new way of living (chapter 11).

## A Problem with This Arrangement

A problem with this arrangement of materials is that it tends to imply more orderliness and uniformity than is true in our experience. Grief is unique in each person and in each situation. No two persons or situations are exactly the same. Grief is seldom simple. It tends to be complex. No one can predict exactly how grief will be experienced by himself or herself, much less by someone else.

The experience of grief is like a walk through a valley. There is more than one entrance and several trails. Even though there can be a variety of causes that send us into the valley, each walk is different because we take different trails or because we focus on different scenes in the valley. Each trip is a unique experience.

Yet the valley is basically the same. In grief there are some basic phases or stages. Sometimes we skip one and dwell on another. But whether we focus on each of them or not, all of the stages described in this book can be found in the valley of grief.

## Varieties of Grief

Usually we think of grief in relation to the death of a person we love. However, other events can cause grief.

Louise did not have many close friends in the small town where she lived. She loved books and ideas and art. Most of the women in her community had never developed these interests. There was one exception, Margret. She was the one person in the town with whom Louise felt close. Then, Margret's husband changed jobs and they moved far away. Louise experienced loss and the anguish of grief.

Bill and Mary were divorced. Although Bill was convinced the divorce was the best solution for everyone concerned, he grieved over the failure of the marriage. He grieved over the loss of a dream.

It was the pocket knife that my grandfather had used as a rancher. I had been very close to my grandfather. The knife was one of the last gifts he gave me. I kept it in my desk drawer and used it to open boxes and letters. One day the knife was gone. It was only a knife but it had special significance to me. I grieved when I lost it.

When I was in high school, the girl I was dating told me that she did not want to "go steady" with me anymore. For days I experienced a terrible ache. Some call that experience "a broken heart." Today I realize I was experiencing grief.

Anytime a significant loss causes us to experience deep sorrow or anguish or remorse, we are in grief. It may be a financial loss, a job loss, the loss of health, the loss of some desired possibilities, the loss of hope, or the loss of a friendship. Grief can be caused by retirement, divorce, or business failure. Any loss that is a significant loss to us personally can trigger the grief experience.

However, when we speak of grief, usually we are refering to the grief we experience when someone we love dies.

This book will focus on grief related to death. However, with only minor modifications, the insights presented in this book can be relevant for any situation of grief.

### Dangers in Grief

Grief can be destructive. Mrs. Martin was very close to her husband. They had been friends, lovers, husband and wife for more than forty years. When Mr. Martin died, Mrs. Martin went into the valley of grief and stayed there. Today, six years later, she is still there. She refuses to mix with other people. She keeps the shades pulled in her house. Her conversations focus on the events of years ago. Like singing the refrain of a song, she says over and over: "I don't know what I'll do without him."

Mr. Lucas is a bitter man. He hates the large company that has employed him the last twenty-five years. He feels the company has ruined his life. Years ago, when Mr. Lucas graduated from college with highest honors, he went to work for this large company and expected quickly to become a top executive. Other people thought the same thing. But something happened. After a few promotions, a position Mr. Lucas really wanted was given to the son of one of the company's vice presidents. Mr. Lucas went into grief and never fully recovered. In his grief he began to withdraw. He felt his dreams crumbling. His humor began to have a cutting, angry edge to it. His bitterness increased.

Grief can be evil; that is, it can be a destructive force, something that tears down life. Grief can rob life of its potential. It can twist healthy personalities into sick distortions.

## My Experience of Grace in Grief

Although grief can be destructive, it does not have to be. God does not abandon us to the destructive power in grief. Throughout the Bible there are many passages that remind us that God's grace is with us. One of the most familiar verses is Psalm 23:4: "Even though I walk through the valley of the shadow of death, I fear no evil [destruction]; for thou art with me; thy rod and thy staff they comfort me." This has been a very meaningful verse for me. It helped me to deal with my grief when Dad died, and thus, come to terms with some of the other griefs in my life.

In this familiar verse, the poet not only says God will be with me in that dark valley, but also gives me some clues about *how* God will be there. God will be there like a shepherd with a rod and a staff, using the tools needed to fight off the wolves. God will be there with the tools needed to push me on when I am ready to quit. God will be there with the tools needed to pull me through the tight places in life.

People have been the tools God has used in my life. They have been like the shepherd's rod and staff. Some people have been used by God to defend me from "wolves" that I did not have sense enough to avoid. Others have been the "shepherd's staff" God has used to pull me through the narrow squeezes in my life. God has worked through persons to protect me and move me through the valley.

"Thy rod and thy staff they comfort me." Comfort is not the same thing as sympathy. A sympathetic person may cry because I am crying; however, a person who comforts me is a person who gives me strength to stand and power to move on. When I am comforted, I discover I have what is needed to face life as it really is and what I need in order to move on in search of positive possibilities. The strength to face reality and the power to move ahead are the basic ingredients in comfort.

When Dad died, I needed comforting. I needed strength to face reality and power to move on. Dad and I always had a good relationship. The year before we discovered he had lung cancer, our relationship had moved to a new level. No longer were we merely father and son; we also discovered respect for each other's professional skills. Just as we were beginning to enjoy this new dimension of our relationship, he died. My grief was severe.

Then the people came with their hugs and kisses and fumbled words. They sent cards, brought cakes, and made awkward visits. Here and there in the midst of all these gestures of sympathy and love, I was comforted. Exactly how it happened is a mystery to me. Two persons could do the same thing; through the actions of one I would receive only sympathy, but through the actions of the other I would find comfort.

It is probably not by accident that the Gospel of John often describes the Holy Spirit as "the Comforter." It is a mystery beyond our control. Jesus told Nicodemus that the work of the Spirit is like the wind; no one can say where it is coming from or where it is going (John 3:8). Likewise, in my grief I could not say when or from whom my comfort would come. But it came—often as a surprise.

Through the words and deeds of my friends, I received comfort. But it was something more than the work of my friends. It was the grace of God. Through their love, God's love was given and I discovered, bit by bit, that I could face my loss and move on. I was comforted.

### An Audacious Claim

It is audacious of me to claim God is active in my life. But this audacity is the stuff proclamation of the Gospel is made of.

Through my experience of grief I gained a new sense of what it means to speak of God at work among us and through us. It was more than the words and deeds of my friends that comforted me. It was the grace of God at work in their love that comforted me.

The grace of God I experienced in my grief, other persons have experienced in theirs. It is these experiences that have led me to believe God's grace can be discovered in all grief. Nothing separates us from the love of God (Rom. 8), not even our grief.

### What Is God's Grace?

In my search to find the best way to describe or define grace, I looked in several books. The best I found was in *The Interpreter's Dictionary of the Bible* (Vol. E—J, page 466):

(1) Grace is a free gift and unearned.

(2) Grace is an abundant gift, a gift far larger than we can ever imagine.

(3) Grace is received through faith.

(4) Grace is an active and effective power from God, bringing merciful aid to persons.

In this book, the fourth statement about grace is the one that is emphasized. Grace is the word I use to point toward the activities of God's love in our lives.

Who can count the ways God reaches out toward us, offering wholeness to our brokenness, fulfillment to our emptiness, purpose to our sense of futility? Grace is the word I use to point toward the mysterious healing, redeeming, reconciling realities at work in our lives. This grace expresses itself in the words and actions of people. It is in the various realities symbolized and expressed in giving a cup of water to the thirsty. This grace also reveals itself in a cluster of meanings we can discover in the sacraments.

This grace is revealed in the stories and insights from the scriptures. This grace is both celebrated and discovered in our various acts of worship. Through the struggles and the calms in a life of prayer, grace comes.

It is no easier to say what grace is than it is to say what a mother's love is. A mother's love is never seen; only the fruits or by-products of her love are visible. We see her taking care of her children; feeding them, nursing them when they are sick, worrying and searching for them when they are lost, scolding and disciplining them when they are misusing their lives. We see only signs of love, and the signs alone are not her love. Her love is more than any expression of it. Her love is invisible. It is beyond measuring, beyond the categories of proof.

God's grace is the activity of God's love. We do not deserve it; we cannot earn it. It is there . . . here . . . then . . . now. Like a mother's love, all we can see are by-products; all we can see are signs. Only through the eyes of faith can the significance of the signs be discovered.

In this book I am making no effort to prove God's grace is active in our lives. This is assumed. What I will do is describe a few situations that may happen as we experience grief and say: "Hey, isn't that one of the fruits of grace? Isn't that another sign of God's love in our lives?"

# ~2~

*Our initial reaction to death is precisely that—our initial reaction. To view it as the true expression of our deepest self is to misunderstand what is happening and to be vulnerable to additional problems.*

# Entering the Valley of Grief

ᘏᘏᘏᘏᘏᘏ

### The Sudden Death

"I was numb. I couldn't believe it. I heard the doctor. My mind comprehended what he was telling me, but I felt as if I were an outside observer. It seemed that this was happening to someone else. I heard him ask me if I was all right and I heard myself say: 'I'm okay; I'll make it.'

"I could see clearly. I could hear. Yet I felt as if I were in a fog. Some of the neighbors were with me. Most of them were crying. I wondered what was wrong with me because I was not crying. After all, Nancy was my wife!

"It seemed an eternity ago that the phone call brought me to the hospital. I looked at my watch; it had only been a couple of hours."

"Nothing we can do," the doctor had said. "Massive head injuries."

"All this cannot be happening . . . but it is. I must make myself think. What do I need to do? Nancy wanted to go out Friday. We will not be doing that . . . I've got to think of other things. What shall I tell the kids? What am I going to do with the children while I am at work? . . . I wonder if we have enough milk at home for their breakfast tomorrow? Nancy took care of things like that.

"I hear myself responding to some friends: 'I know it has happened. It just does not seem real.' "

~ 23 ~

Our initial reaction to an unexpected death is usually one of shock and numbness. However, our initial reaction to an anticipated death is different. If the process of dying has been prolonged, the reaction tends to be one of relief.

### The Prolonged Death

*Thank God it's over.* The thought played in her mind like a stuck record.

How long had it been? Mrs. Wallace had lost track of the days, the weeks, the months. For a while her father would be in a nursing home, and then he would be back in the hospital. The cycle was repeated again and again. It seemed like an endless treadmill between the hospital and the nursing home.

Mrs. Wallace had watched her father change from a strong, independent person into a weak and helpless "infant." She saw him change from a person who enjoyed life and people into a person who was suspicious and afraid. Although she had responsibilities for her children and a part-time job, Mrs. Wallace visited him at least once a day, usually twice. But he became forgetful, and he would forget her having been to see him. Several times he was angry with her and accused her of not caring. He even believed she did not care. In tears he told her that he wished he could die and not be a bother to her any more. Little by little, he lost touch with reality. His mind returned to his past. He relived events and conversations that had taken place many years ago. Toward the end, he even lost touch with the past. He lay in bed and stared blankly into space.

It was painful to Mrs. Wallace to watch her father's mind and body deteriorate. The process of his dying was so slow. Finally death came.

Exhausted physically and emotionally, Mrs. Wallace felt as if a huge weight had been lifted from her shoulders. She felt so relieved that she worried about herself: "What is wrong with me? I loved Dad. Shouldn't I feel more sadness? All I feel is relief. If I feel anything it is more of a feeling of gladness. I'm glad my ordeal is over. . . . Is that wrong?"

*Gifts and Problems*

Our initial responses to a significant loss can be viewed as gifts. When death is a sudden, unexpected event, our numbness can be seen as a gift of calmness that will allow us to absorb what has happened; it even allows us to take care of some practical questions before we are hit by the emotional storms. When the death has been anticipated for some time, the relief we may experience can be understood as the gift of a brief rest between two ordeals: the ordeal of anticipating a significant loss and the ordeal of adjusting to the implications that loss has for our living. Thus, the first stage or phase of grief can be seen as a gift of God's grace.

However, we sometimes have problems in this first part of our grief experience. Sometimes the problems stem from our misunderstanding our feelings, and sometimes the problems stem from our reactions to what people around us say and do.

If we view our initial reaction to death as our total response, we may be in for some problems. Taken out of the context of the total grief experience, our initial reaction may cause us to enter grief with a low opinion of ourselves. For example, if we think that our initial reaction of numbness is our primary experience of grief, we are likely to view ourselves as being insensitive. If we think that our initial reaction of relief is our primary experience of grief, we are likely to view ourselves as selfish, unloving persons. If this happens we add the burden of low self-esteem to the burden of our grief.

Our initial reaction to death is precisely that—our initial reaction. To view it as the true expression of our deepest self is to misunderstand what is happening and to be vulnerable to additional problems.

In this situation we may also misunderstand other people's attempts to help us. In their desire to be helpful and supportive, they will sometimes view the exterior behavior of our initial response and make comments such as: "You are so strong!" or "I certainly admire the way you are taking this"; or "For you to be so calm, your faith must be very deep."

If we are already feeling some form of mild guilt because we misunderstand our numbness or relief, these well-intentioned compliments may pour more fuel on our fires of guilt. They tell us we are strong and that we have faith, but we see ourselves as being insensitive and selfish. In this situation the compliments make us feel guilty because of the gap between their description of us and our image of ourselves.

If we listen *only* to the words our friends say, their comments are likely to be misunderstood. If that happens, their gestures of friendship will be significantly less helpful than they were intended to be.

"You are so strong!" may say to us: "Hold all your emotion in; do not let it splash on other people."

"I certainly admire the way you are taking this," may say to us: "I accept your grief so long as it does not bother me. Keep it to yourself."

"Your faith is so strong!" may say to us: "It is your Christian duty to be a silent, smiling rock. Faith does not know sorrow."

When we listen only to the words of our friends, we are setting ourselves up for misunderstanding. If we listen only to their words and are not sensitive to the concern and love behind their words, we are likely to miss the message our friends are attempting to express. And when we misunderstand the comments, we are likely to be caught somewhere between not liking ourselves (because we are not living up to what we think is their image of us) and trying to act like the person we think they want us to be. The result of these misunderstandings is a loss of intimacy that tends to make us feel isolated rather than comforted. Later, during the emotional storms of sorrow and anguish when we need to reach out to others, we may feel cut off.

To prevent this from happening, we need to see our initial reaction to loss as only the first phase of grief, and we need to be sensitive to the love behind our friends' words. Our friends are not trying to set us up as ideal superhumans. They are not trying to cut us off. They are reaching out in love to give us support. We need to be sensitive to their intentions. It is the reality of their love—more than their particular words or deeds—that gives us what we need in our grief.

### Grace and Faith

When we are touched by the love of our friends, we are also touched by the grace of God. We receive all this love by faith. We trust that we are loved; it is a leap of faith. We trust that somewhere within the poorly chosen words and awkward acts, is the love our friends offer to us. We have no illusions that the love we receive from our friends is totally free from their self-interest, but also we are free from the disillusion that focuses only on the self-interest and imperfection that are there. Within the faults, failures, and sins of our neighbors are also their genuine attempts to love. By faith we receive their words and deeds, focusing on the element (sometimes only a trace) of love that is there.

Within the love that comes from our friends, there is the grace of God, that source of strength which enables us to face what has to be faced and that also gives us the power to move on. This reality is a mystery. It cannot be proven to the skeptic (a fact which is frustrating to both the skeptic and the faithful). Just as a mother's love cannot be finally proven and just as the love of a friend can be perceived only through faith, so also the grace of God cannot be proven to someone who is committed to the belief that God's love is only a sentimental illusion.

God's grace is as real as the love of family and friends. In truth, God's grace is in (but not limited to) the love of family and friends. It is freely given to provide us what we need in our grief. It takes only the eyes of faith to see it.

# ~3~

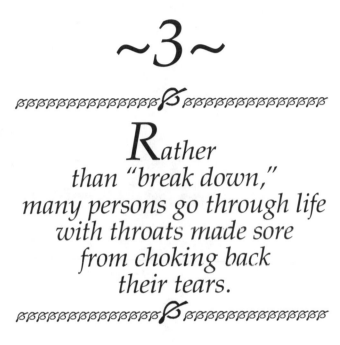

*R*ather
than "break down,"
many persons go through life
with throats made sore
from choking back
their tears.

# The Emotional Storm

*ᏠᏠᏠᏠ ᏠᏠᏠ*

There is an emotional storm within the grief process. It happens when we realize how much we miss the person who is dead. It happens when we begin to sense how much we are going to miss that person in the future. It happens when we realize that some hopes and dreams we had which were related to that person will never be fulfilled. It happens when it dawns on us that a person who has been a vital part of our lives is now only a memory for us. When the news of the death has moved from being information in our heads and has become reality we feel in the pit of our stomachs, we experience the emotional storm of grief.

The storm rages inside us. There is hurt, ache, feelings of emptiness, turmoil of emotions deep within us. There is no one way we express these emotions of grief. Some of us reach out to be held while we weep. Others of us seek solitude for the shedding of tears. Some of us cry like a baby in pain. Others of us sob softly like a child who is lost and afraid. The weeping of some is as silent as a rock and only the flow of tears tells others of the anguish. Some of us talk to ourselves. Others of us cry out to the one who is dead. Still others of us talk to friends, our words tumbling over one another as if projected outward by some powerful inner pressure. Others of us sit in silence.

It is normal to feel the pain of grief and it is healthy to give these feelings some form of expression. In fact it is dangerous to try to deny these feelings. Our feelings are a powerful part of us. When we attempt to deny the reality of our feelings by trying to keep them bottled up, we often discover our unexpressed feelings are shaping all that we think and say and do. Thus, the attempt to control our feelings by denying them, more often than not, results in our feelings controlling us.

Unfortunately, many persons in our culture try to hide or deny the emotional storm in their grief. We are encouraged in this denial by at least three factors or attitudes at work within our society.

### The Temptation to Deny Sadness

One attitude is that happiness is good but sadness is bad. This is the undercurrent theme in many advertisements. The goal in life for many persons is the pursuit of a happiness in which no sadness can be found. They want to avoid sadness, and they tempt us to hide our sorrow. Without intending to hurt us, they make us feel "bad" because we are feeling sad. Because of this extra load they place on our grief, they tempt us to pretend (to ourselves and to them) that we are not grieving.

### The Temptation to Deny Death

Another attitude that encourages us to keep our emotional storm bottled inside ourselves is our culture's tendency to deny death. Only within the last few years have we begun to realize that the subject of death has been as much a taboo in our society as the subject of sex was in the society of Queen Victoria.

Our culture tends to view life as if it were a melodrama in which the hero (or the cavalry) rides in for the rescue just before all is lost. Not only does this attitude make it difficult for us to deal with terminal illness, it makes it difficult for us to deal with grief.

In some ways this attitude is a reflection of one of the strengths within our culture. We are known for our optimism, our unwillingness to admit defeat. This is a great strength and one we need to hold. It is the strength of hope and confidence. But this hope and confidence needs to come to terms with reality. All too often in our society we use the attitude of optimism to hide from realities that frighten us. We dream that if we keep "the right thought," the disturbing reality will go away. This denial of disturbing realities is neither confidence nor hope; it is escapism. This superficial optimism within our culture tempts us to deny any final frustrations, especially the final frustrations of death.

Many of us refuse to think or talk about death. It is as if we believe death will go away if we ignore it. This attitude toward death encourages us to deny our grief.

Even within our churches, we sometimes deny death. For example, in some Protestant churches, the people go straight from the Palm Sunday celebrations of triumph to celebrations of the greater triumph in Easter. They tend to give little more than a passing glance to the reality described in The Apostles' Creed that states, ". . . he was crucified, dead, and buried. . . . " It is tempting to be in such a hurry to be assured of our immortality that we run past the reality of death.

When we are in grief, the people who are near us have to deal with the reality of death. This makes some of them uncomfortable. They do not want to die, nor do they want anyone else to die. They want death to go away. Thus, they quickly proclaim to us what they have half heard in churches and speak to themselves as much as to us who are in grief, saying: "Oh, don't grieve. He is not really dead." Rather than enabling us to cope with our grief, they encourage us to deny what we feel.

### The Temptation to Deny Weakness

Not only do we have outside forces or attitudes tempting us to bottle our emotional storms, but also we have an inner force at work. This inner force is the fear of showing weakness. We do not want to admit our need or dependence.

This fear causes many of us to hide our feelings. We are afraid of being "too emotional." Many men in our society have been taught that "a real man" does not show his feelings. We have been taught it is a sign of weakness to cry. In fact if a man happens to cry, it is usually described as "he broke down." To call crying "breaking down" is to imply something negative about weeping. Rather than "break down," many persons go through life with throats made sore from choking back their tears.

### Grief Is a Sign of Love

> Then Mary, when she came where Jesus was and saw him, fell at his feet, saying to him, "Lord, if you had been here, my brother [Lazarus] would not have died." When Jesus saw her weeping and the Jews who came with her also weeping, he was deeply moved in spirit and troubled . . . Jesus wept. So the Jews said, "See how he loved him!"
> (John 11:32-36)

Tears are okay. They are not a sign of weakness. Death, disappointment, loss, and blocked possibilities cause us to feel anguish. These feelings of pain in our grief are signs of our love. Jesus wept at the death of Lazarus. He did not try to hide his feelings, but the Son of God revealed his vulnerability to being hurt. Jesus revealed his love. His tears were a sign of his love both for Lazarus and the family and friends of Lazarus. The scripture states that "Jesus was troubled and his spirit was deeply moved." He loved. He cared. Jesus wept out of the strength of his love.

One way to view our grief is to see it as the reaction of love to loss. In the Book of Samuel, David experienced this loss. His son, Absalom, tried to overthrow his father's government. David loved his son and undoubtedly had dreams for Absalom and for their relationship. Absalom, however, rejected his father and his father's dreams. In the process, Absalom was killed. David grieved for all he lost. David grieved over (1) the loss of his son, (2) the loss of his dreams for his son, and (3) the loss of the possibility for reconciliation with his son. "O my son Absalom, my son, my son Absalom!" wept David (2 Sam. 18:33).

Why do we weep? We weep because a relationship that nourished our lives has ended. We weep because a person who enabled us to feel needed no longer needs us. We weep because the potential we saw in that relationship died when the person died. We weep because the reconciliation we longed for is no longer possible. All of these—being nourished, being needed, seeing potential, longing for reconciliation—are dimensions of love. If we had no love, we would not grieve. And to deny our grief is to deny our love.

### Grief Is a Sign of Our Humanity

Our pain in grief is also a sign of our humanity. Children cry because a toy is lost or because a toy is broken or because the promised toy is denied. They do not hide their hurt when they experience a significant loss. They expose their vulnerability. They not only expose their hurt; they reveal their need to be comforted, that is, their need to be given strength to face their loss and the power to move on.

To deny our pain in grief is to deny our humanity. All of us are children. All of us are vulnerable. Yet there is something within us that makes us want to deny vulnerability. We want to hide our hurts. Is not this denial a sign of pride? Is not this hiding of our feelings an expression of dishonesty? Is it not playing games to try to hide our grief?

### The Danger

Some persons will say: "But we do not want to indulge in excessive emotionalism. We do not want to fall into self-pity." This may be a problem for some, but we who use these statements to justify our denial of feelings are hardly in danger of excessive emotionalism. The danger we are in is the danger that comes from hiding our true feelings. When we hide our true feelings, we cut ourselves off from significant relationships; we block our ability to receive and give love.

### Being Open to Grace

God made us human beings capable of love and thus capable of grief. God provides us with the grace we need for both love and grief. However, as long as we try to pretend we are self-sufficient, it is difficult for us to receive the grace God is offering. In our self-sufficiency we shut the door on other people, and in turn we shut the door on God's grace because God's grace usually comes to us through the words and deeds of others. If we focus on trying to prove to ourselves and others that we need no one, we will not see or receive the grace that is offered. In our pride we will have blocked our access to the love we need.

God's grace is most effective in our lives when we do not play games with ourselves or with God. God's love is always reaching out to us, but if we are unwilling to admit our hurts and needs, we are turning our backs on God's out-stretched arms.

When we do not try to hide our feelings from ourselves or from our friends, we are more likely to be aware of our inadequacies, and we are more willing to admit our need for help. It is this awareness, this openness, this need that enables us to receive the grace God is continually offering.

To discover God's grace in our grief, we have to admit our need to ourselves and to others. The emotional storm can be seen not only as an expression of our love for what we lost, but also as the catalyst that enables us to face and admit our human limitations, vulnerability, and need. Grace can be seen in whatever sets us on the road to seeking God's help.

# ~4~

*As we tell each other our memories, we can discover inner strength growing within us. God's grace is at work in this sharing that gives us strength.*

# Nostalgia in Grief

*Remember When . . .*

When Dad died, our family gathered and friends came by. We were drawn together by the power love has when it becomes grief. Each of us had been touched by Dad's life. Now he was dead and we would miss him. The closer we were to him, the greater our pain.

United in our grief, we felt close to one another. The distinction between friends and family seemed to melt. Affection and sympathy urged us to touch each other. When we shook hands there was an added touch. More often than usual we would embrace and kiss. Sometimes this was done in silence, our tears speaking for us. Sometimes someone said: "I'm sorry"; or "Is there anything we can do?" or simply "Oh, Jim . . ."

Once we passed the initial greeting, we expressed the love that brought us together by talking about Dad. It was not a planned or calculated ritual. It was the natural thing to do. Without realizing how we started, my mother or one of my sisters or I would discover ourselves retelling the story of Dad's dying. We seemed compelled to tell it and those who came seemed eager—not just eager, needing—to hear it. Over and over we told the story of the medical examination, the grim report, our difficulty believing the bad news, the efforts to find a cure, the bravery of Dad, the ordeals in the hospital, and finally the story about the night he died.

After some comments or questions, the conversation usually drifted toward some pleasant memories: "Remember the time he took us fishing?" or "Remember how he loved watermelon? Well, one time . . ." or "Did I ever tell you about the time he . . ."

Sometimes our memories were triggered by someone who was present. "Isn't that John Roberts in the kitchen? I remember one time when your dad and John . . ."

We shared our memories. Many of them caused us to smile or laugh. Sometimes the memories woke such feelings of affection or pride that tears came, and it was difficult to talk. In all this it was as if we had an inner compulsion to remind ourselves about who Dad was and what he meant to our lives. At other times it seemed we used our conversations as a way to allow the reality of his death to soak in.

Not all of our memories were pleasant. Dad died in my arms, struggling for breath. That experience was not a pleasant one. As I moved beyond the first days of grief, I remembered ways I had let Dad down. I remembered childhood lies I told. I remembered his anger toward me when he blamed me for breaking a tool I had not broken or even used. I remembered from childhood how I resented Dad not taking time to hike with me the way my friend's father did with his sons. Dad always seemed too busy to play. Not all memories are pleasant.

Why does grief trigger so much remembering? There are several factors that rouse our memories. Our daily routine is interrupted, and our attention is focused on one specific part of our life. The spotlight of our emotions is on a specific relationship. Even after the funeral when we return to our routine responsibilities, our emotional focus is on what we have lost. Whenever the demand of our daily responsibilities lets up, our thoughts seem pulled to the source of our grief and we "remember when."

Death often puts us in contact with persons from our past. Family members and friends we have not seen or heard from in a long time visit or write or call. These people from our past wake sleeping memories. Events and experiences that we have not thought about in years flood our minds. Remembering is stimulated even more by our conversations. We talk about the past experiences we share. We retell old memories with people we have not seen for a long time.

## The Danger in Our Memories

Grief stimulates a lot of remembering. Some of this remembering is pleasant, some is not. The concern is not whether we will do a lot of remembering. Nor is it whether we will have more pleasant than unpleasant memories. The concern is whether our memories will be positive or negative forces in our living. Our pleasant and unpleasant memories either help free us to move on, or they become chains holding us back.

Our pleasant memories can shackle us to the past. In chapter 1 the experience of Mrs. Martin was described. When her husband died, she went into grief and never came out. She allowed her pleasant memories to hold her back. She had good memories about their marriage. The more she focused on how good the old days were with him, the more she dreaded facing new days without him. The more she focused on how much she had depended on him, the more she doubted she could make it by herself. Her pleasant memories created the illusion of a safe, secure, and happy past that she did not want to leave.

Pleasant memories tempt us to idealize the past. This idealized illusion of yesterday tempts us to hang on to what is dead and gone. If we become slaves to our pleasant memories, we will overlook the life that is possible for us today.

Unpleasant memories can be a negative force also. These memories have two sources: ourselves and the person who died. When the source of our unpleasant memories is ourselves, we remember the errors we made or the hurts we caused or the good we failed to do. When the source of our unpleasant memories is the person who died, we remember the errors and the hurts he or she caused.

Our unpleasant memories are a negative force in our lives when we allow them to reinforce a low opinion of ourselves. For example, Mary remembers the arguments she had with her father. It was difficult for them to visit without having a disagreement that caused tempers to flare. If they had a peaceful visit, it was because both of them avoided all the sensitive topics or because they were less than candid with one another.

Mary remembers the hurt she caused her father. She remembers her anger toward her father. She remembers how their relationship was and she blames herself. The ache in her grief is compounded by her reinforced low opinion of herself. She accuses herself of being excessively insensitive and selfish. Her regret over what she did and what she failed to do carries the weight of guilt. When she dreams about the relationship that might have been (perhaps could have been), her regret becomes self-contempt.

Not all of her unpleasant memories are "her fault." Some of the unpleasant memories are of her father hurting her. For example, Mary's feelings were hurt by her father in an argument. In his anger he told her he did not think she would ever amount to much as a teacher. He accused her of being insensitive, impractical, and hot-headed. "All you can do is hurt people," he said. Mary remembers and the pain of her grief is increased with the burden of self-doubt. She allows this negative memory to reinforce a low opinion of herself. Because unpleasant memories are painful, we are tempted to deny them. We are certainly tempted to deny an unpleasant memory about someone we have loved. If we care enough about someone to experience grief when he or she dies, we do not want the person's faults and failures to be what we remember.

The danger in denying unpleasant memories is at least twofold: (1) if we idealize the past, we can become emotionally chained to it; (2) if we idealize the person who died, we can experience feelings of insecurity ("I cannot make it without him") and/or self-contempt ("It was all my fault").

### *Grace in Remembering and in the Memory*

In grief we find ourselves doing a lot of remembering. Remembering does not have to be a negative force. It can be one of the tools God uses to enable us to face our loss. Memories can be a source of strength enabling us to move on. God's grace can come to us through this part of our grief experience.

We are united with friends and family members as we share our memories. Our sharing can tie us together and help us feel less vulnerable. As we tell each other our memories, we can discover inner strength growing within us. God's grace is at work in this sharing that gives us strength. God's grace is at work in whatever enables us to realize that we are not totally alone.

Inner strength also comes from the memories themselves. Thus God uses both the act of remembering and our memories to give the grace we need.

It is easy to see how grace comes through our pleasant memories. From them we discover some of the good gifts that have come into our lives for which we can be thankful. As we remember the good times, we can rediscover experiences in life that make living a joy. This can influence us to rearrange our priorities. As we see good aspects of our relationship with the one who died, we become more aware of the great potential in all our relationships. The awareness of this potential can excite us to improve our relations with others.

When people talked about Tom's father, the memories seemed to illustrate how hard he tried to be fair and just in all situations. This was a characteristic that Tom admired. Remembering the example set by his father, Tom rededicated himself to be that kind of example for his son.

Even our unpleasant memories can be a means of grace. As we remember the imperfections in our relationship, we can obtain wisdom. In our unpleasant memories we can find the resolve we need to change patterns in our behavior. Unpleasant memories can be God's gift that causes us to change and become better persons. For example, Tom remembered how much he wanted his father to play with him, but his father was always too busy. At times Tom felt his father had rejected him. Thus, Tom gained wisdom from this unpleasant memory and vowed to make time for his son.

## The Significance of Seeking

What is the factor that makes our remembering a positive force? What keeps our remembering from being a negative power in our grief? The answer to this mystery includes something about our expectations. Discovering grace in our memories is related to whether or not we are looking for it. "Blessed are those who hunger and thirst for righteousness, for they shall be satisfied," Jesus said (Matt. 5:6). We who long for, who look for (who hunger and thirst for) a good relationship with God (righteousness) are going to be satisfied. That is the promise in this beatitude.

We can do something to facilitate our ability to receive the grace God is giving. "Seek, and you will find . . ." Jesus said (Matt. 7:7). Without questioning that we are saved by grace through faith, we can recognize the necessity of our participation.

Discovering grace in our "remembering when . . ." is related to what we are looking for in our memories. If we are not looking for a pearl, we are likely to swallow it with the oyster. If we are looking for the grace of God, it seems that we will be more likely to recognize it when it comes to us. And it will come. The grace of God is at work in all things, even our "remembering when . . ."

# ~5~

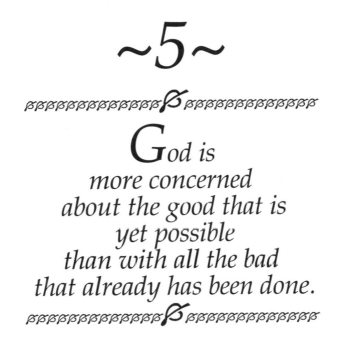

God is
more concerned
about the good that is
yet possible
than with all the bad
that already has been done.

# Feeling Guilty

It is not unusual in grief to feel guilty. Sometimes we can identify what is causing our guilt feelings and sometimes we cannot. All we know is that we feel "it" is our fault. We feel that we have failed to be the persons we should have been. We do not like ourselves and in our state of feeling guilty it is difficult for us to believe God or anyone else could love us if he or she really knew us. In the self contempt of our guilt we have great difficulty accepting or giving affection. Our feelings of guilt cut us off from the love we need.

This chapter has two goals: one is to point to some of the sources of our guilt feelings and the other is to point to some of the ways God's grace comes when we feel guilty.

### Sources of Feeling Guilty

Some of our guilt feelings are related to something we did (or failed to do) years ago. These negative feelings are by-products of the unpleasant memories discussed in the previous chapter. Mary felt guilty when she remembered some of the ways she hurt her father.

Some of our guilt feelings are related to our low opinion of ourselves. Joe did not feel his life was much of a success. He was not sure what "success" was, but he felt he had not achieved it. Joe thought that his father had been disappointed in him. When his father died, Joe felt a sense of guilt and self-contempt.

Sometimes the shock of a death and the anguish of grief can release repressed guilt. This guilt has waited a long time for some event to turn it loose. This happened to Nancy when her best friend, Rachel, died. Nancy experienced feelings of guilt, but she could not figure out why. Her friendship with Rachel was almost ideal. One day while watching a soap opera, Nancy realized the source of her guilt feeling. Twenty years ago Nancy had an affair with another friend's husband. Her friend found out, and their friendship ended. Nancy was in grief over the loss of her friend and her lover. She felt guilty because of all the pain she helped create, but she did not work through her grief or her guilt. She repressed it. All this happened years before Nancy met Rachel. Nancy's grief over Rachel's death released the feelings of grief and guilt she had repressed twenty years ago.

Sometimes the guilt feelings are related directly to the death. In one situation, a twelve-year-old boy accidentally hanged himself. He was standing on a ladder tying a rope to a tree limb. Somehow he knocked the ladder over and became entangled in the rope and strangled. No one knows exactly how it happened. The parents of this boy had strong guilt feelings. The father said: "If only I had thrown away that old rope." The mother added: "And if only I had gone outside a few minutes earlier."

In another situation a father accidentally shot and killed his son. In yet another situation a teenager was driving and had an accident in which his mother was killed. In these and similar situations, the feelings of grief were accompanied by self-accusation and strong feelings of guilt. Whenever we can see some clear connection between the death and what we did (or failed to do), our grief carries a heavy load of guilt.

It is not unusual for us to search for something to feel guilty about. This search for "What I did wrong" is sometimes related to our fears and doubts about ourselves. It is as if we are looking for something that will confirm our low opinion of ourselves.

Then, too, it is difficult for us to stand in the wake of a tragedy with all of its unanswered questions. We believe if we could find some cause, something that went wrong, someone to blame, the tragedy would be more acceptable. It is so difficult to live with unanswered questions regarding tragedies that we sometimes assume the burden of guilt to have "a reason why."

A woman whose husband died of a sudden heart attack blamed herself for not having forced him to take better care of himself. A man whose wife died unexpectedly kept asking himself: "Isn't there something I could have done?"

Our low opinion of ourselves and our longing for an answer will even tempt us to view our loss as some form of punishment. This was Bill's temptation. His wife died a slow death. She was only twenty-six when she died and left Bill with a four-year-old girl. Bill had to struggle with the suspicion that her suffering and death were somehow his fault. He was tempted, like Job, to believe his loss and sorrow were some sort of punishment. By assuming the blame there would be an explanation, a reason, a purpose for all his anguish. If he assumed the guilt, he would not have to cope with the profound mysteries of unexplainable suffering. He was tempted to assume the blame and thus create the illusion of understanding why it had all happened.

In the story of Adam and Eve, God forbids them to eat the fruit of one tree, "the tree of the knowledge of good and evil" (Gen. 2–3). In Gerhard von Rad's book, *Genesis—A Commentary* (published by The Westminster Press, 1972), the author states that the phrase "good and evil" as it is used in this story is a Hebrew expression that means "everything." Thus the tree was the tree of knowing everything. In telling them not to eat the fruit of this tree, God was telling Adam and Eve to refrain from trying to be "know-it-alls." God was telling Adam and Eve that they could fulfill their place in the creation only by coming to terms with their basic human limitations. The desire to be "know-it-alls" (the desire to be like the Creator rather than like creatures) would destroy them.

In the wake of a tragedy with all its unanswerable questions, we are tempted to assume guilt. This guilt is an attempt to furnish ourselves with explanations. Instead of facing the dark, unanswerable mysteries in human suffering, we do what Adam and Eve did. We try to be like God.

We have pointed to five sources of guilt: (1) our memories, especially unpleasant ones (see chapter 4); (2) our low opinion of ourselves, which is sometimes coupled with (3) repressed guilts; (4) our seeing some connection between what we did (or failed to do) and the death; and (5) our preference to assume guilt rather than cope with unanswerable mysteries regarding human suffering.

### Grace in Discovering the Cause

One of the ways God's grace is at work in this phase of our grief is in helping us to identify the source of our guilt. Sometimes merely realizing what is causing us to feel guilty will free us from those negative feelings. This is usually the case when the guilt is an inappropriate guilt that we have been taught to feel. For example, Louise felt guilty after her father died. She did not know why. She guessed it was part of her grief, but that realization did not relieve her from the burden of feeling she had done something wrong. In a conversation with a friend, the cause of her guilt came out. She was talking about her father's funeral: "Everything was just the way he wanted it . . . except he did not die at home with his family around him. He had often said that is the way he wanted to go. He died with strangers in an intensive care unit in the hospital."

No sooner had she spoken than she realized his dying away from home was the cause for her feeling she had done something wrong. Obviously she had done nothing wrong. She knew she had done the best she could for her father. The mere awareness of what was behind her guilt feelings released her. She regretted her father's wish had not been fulfilled, but there is a vast difference between regret over someone's wish not coming true and the self-contempt of "It's my fault."

God's grace is at work in all the ways we are helped to identify the source of our guilt feelings. Sometimes identifying the source of our guilt is enough to release us from feeling guilty. However, this identification is usually just the first step toward accepting forgiveness. This first step is quite a gift! Anyone who has experienced the anguish of seemingly sourceless self-contempt knows just how big a gift it really is. As long as we cannot identify the cause of our guilt feelings, we have little hope of being released from our sense of guilt.

Knowledge of what is causing us to feel guilty usually is not enough. The writer of Psalm 51:3 knew what was causing him to feel guilty: "For I know my transgressions, and my sin is ever before me." His past haunted him; he could not get away from it. It may be so with us. Identification of the cause of guilt may not release us from our self-contempt. We are stuck with the awareness that we have failed to be the persons we wished we had been. We do not like ourselves, and it is difficult for us to believe God or others could love us if they really knew us. Sometimes this self-contempt is so severe that we withdraw from people and thus move away from the sources of God's healing grace.

### Grace in Our Yearnings

One of the ways God's grace is at work is in our yearning to be at peace with ourselves.

Robert felt sick when he remembered what he had done. How could he have allowed himself to cause so much pain? If only there was something he could do. He longed to have the self-respect he had once enjoyed. He longed to be able to look his neighbors in the face without feeling guilty. Finally, he could not keep it all bottled inside himself. His aches and longings drove him to seek some advice from a friend. His yearnings for wholeness and peace sent him outside himself.

There is a longing to be in harmony with life. It is a longing to be able to love and to be loved. It is a yearning for wholeness and peace and fulfillment. This yearning is a gift God's grace has placed within us. This yearning is one of the doors God has given us for grace to come through.

When we are captives of our guilt, God's grace comes to us in the form of mercy. When our guilt has locked us inside ourselves, God's mercy comes seeking us through the doorway of our deepest yearnings.

### Mercy

To speak of God's mercy is not to speak of a sentimental attitude that does not care about the abuses of yesterday. To be merciful is to do something more profound than to overlook wrong. To be merciful is to do something more than simply not care how rotten a person was in the past.

Nor is it to play a game of pretending the past wrongs never happened.

Mercy cares. Mercy restores relationships. Mercy cares about the wrong that was done, but it cares more about the potential for good that remains. Out of its awareness of what can be, mercy restores relationship.

The motivation to be merciful does not come from focusing on the past. It comes from focusing on the present and future possibilities. I have never been able to be merciful when I was focusing on the wrong that was done yesterday. It was only when I was able to sense the positive potential and possibilities in today and tomorrow that I was able to be merciful. God sees the positive potential in each of us. That is, God is more concerned about the good that is yet possible than with all the bad that already has been done.

This is true even though the good that seems possible appears so small in comparison with the wrong that has been done. God does not view life the way we do. Jesus said to the thief on the cross: "Today you will be with me in Paradise" (Luke 23:43). Christ cared more about fulfilling the potential for good in that moment than he did about all the past wrongs the thief had done. To be sure, the thief did not escape the consequences of his yesterdays (nor do we). He was still a thief being executed on a cross. Yet in that situation, with all of its severe limitations, God was concerned for the thief to fulfill his remaining potential. God was more concerned about the relationship that could be than with past wrongs.

To say that God is merciful is to acknowledge that God's focus is not on the past. God's focus is on the possibilities of fulfilling the best that is within us now. Even if "now" we are like that thief dying on his cross, we are still important to God.

In our grief we need to receive the grace of God's mercy. It is very easy for us to become locked in the prison of remembering our failures. It is very easy for us to allow our abuses of the past to fill us with feelings of guilt. Caught in the web of guilt, we miss the possibilities that are present today. We need to receive God's mercy that focuses on the present, positive potential. We need to receive this mercy from God so that we can be merciful to ourselves. With this mercy, we can look into our own lives and see what God sees there—positive potential.

### How Grace Comes

How does this aspect of God's grace come to us? The primary instrument God uses to give us grace is other people. It comes through what they do; sometimes it comes through what they refuse to do—the burdens they refuse to put on our backs. It comes through their compassion and love; it comes through their knowledge and the insights they share. God uses people who are near us and people who live far away. God uses people we love and people we hardly know. God's grace comes through words people have written. It even comes through the memory of persons we have not seen for years.

Sometimes it is the memory of other persons and their faith that keeps us going. Earlier a verse from Psalm 51 was quoted. The poet (some say it was David) was caught in the agony of guilt. One of the ways grace came to him was in the memory of a promise: "a broken and contrite heart, O God, thou wilt not despise" (Psalm 51:17). Even though he did not yet feel the release of forgiveness, he found strength to endure by remembering the promise of forgiveness.

One of the ways God's grace comes to us in the midst of our guilt feelings is in our remembering the promises of the Gospel. Jesus said: "For where two or three are gathered in my name, there am I in the midst of them" (Matt.18:20). He said this while talking to the disciples about forgiveness. Whatever else this passage may mean, it clearly implies that Christ—the grace of God—comes to us through each other.

We can relate the presence of Christ—the presence of grace—to the phrase "gathered in my name." To be gathered in the name of Christ is something more profound than meeting together under a Christian label. For the Jews of Bible times the word *name* referred to more than a label. It referred to the essence, the basic quality, the identifying reality. Thus, a group that is gathered in the name of Christ has the basic quality that identified Christ, namely the love of God.

We are most likely to receive grace, especially grace in the form of forgiveness or mercy, in a group marked by the love of God. This group may or may not talk a lot about Jesus, but it will definitely be a group in which there is the kind of love that identified Jesus as the Christ. It will be a group "gathered in my name."

Sometimes we find this group within a congregation, among peers at work or friends in the neighborhood, or just between us and one other person. Sometimes the grace of God comes through the people we expected it to come through; sometimes we are quite surprised by the persons God uses to deliver grace to us.

Since we can never say in advance who God is going to use to deliver grace, we dare not shut ourselves off from people or allow ourselves to give in to the feelings of self-contempt. People are the primary instruments God uses to deliver us from our distress.

One more practical word needs to be stated. Sometimes we have special needs. Sometimes our feelings of guilt continue to plague us for a long time. When this happens, it may be a signal that we need to seek trained help. In almost every community there is at least one pastor who has developed special counseling skills. Most pastors know psychologists or psychiatrists who can help. The availability of these persons is another expression of God's grace.

# ~6~

*The temptation to quit can be strong. When we are ready to give up, we need to draw on resources outside ourselves. In such times it is necessary to turn to God and to others.*

# Grief's Physical Impact
ʚʚʚ β ʚʚʚ

### A Two-Way Street

*He grieved himself sick. She died of a broken heart.* There is some basis for these two folk-observations. We are unified human beings; our bodies are not isolated from our emotions. The condition of our bodies can influence how we cope with our emotions; it can even influence the emotions we experience. Our emotional condition can influence our physical health. It is a two-way street.

"I'm not hungry. Since Louise died, I just do not have an appetite. I don't know how long it has been since I really slept. Oh, I sleep but it is a restless sleep. I am up and down all night. When I am asleep, I dream and dream. When I wake, I do not feel rested."

"Is there some medical reason why persons who have experienced intense grief quite often become ill?" The pastor was talking with his physician. "I have noticed that it is not unusual for persons who have been in grief for some time to become so sick that they have to be placed in a hospital."

In this chapter we will first look at how grief can have a negative impact on our eating, resting, and exercise. Second, we will look at how these three deficiencies can become a destructive spiral. Third, we will explore how grace is related to this aspect of grief.

## Loss of Appetite

Many persons lose their appetites in periods of grief. This loss may be attributed to many things. For some of us, the focus is on concerns other than food; we are distracted. For others, mealtime used to be a special time that was enjoyed with the one who is now dead. Now that this relationship has been broken by death, meals are avoided in a subconscious effort to avoid remembering how much has been lost. Perhaps a loss of appetite is related to a general loss of the will to live. The person who died was so important to us that we do not have a strong desire to continue. Of course, some combination of these three reasons could be the cause or it might be some other reason entirely. Regardless of the precise cause, if we do not eat properly our physical health will deteriorate.

## Loss of Sleep

Some of us in the emotional stress of grief have difficulty sleeping. Perhaps this difficulty in going to sleep is related to some unrecognized fear of death. Or, maybe we are worried about how we are going to face the future without this person on whom we have relied so heavily. When we try to sleep, our minds seem to raise one potential problem after another; instead of sleeping we lie in bed worrying.

It is not unusual for persons who are in grief to dream more than they normally do. Sometimes this dreaming can contribute to restless sleep. If the dreams are unpleasant, we may avoid bedtime and try to get by on as little sleep as possible. When we do not get enough rest, we run down our bodies and lower our resistance to disease.

### Lack of Exercise

In grief we often neglect physical exercise. Other concerns have our attention. Or we say we. do not feel like exercising. A lack of exercise can cause us to be sluggish. It can also contribute to our loss of appetite and our inability to rest.

### Grief and Health Problems

It is not surprising that persons in grief often become physically ill. Having neglected food, sleep, and exercise, they become run-down and easy victims for the first disease that comes along.

The loss of physical health often adds to the emotional stress in grief. When we are in poor physical health, we are less able to cope with our emotional problems. In fact, poor physical health may cause more emotional problems.

### A Destructive Spiral

Sometimes grief tempts us to give up. We have the tendency to face each day with an attitude of "Why bother any more?" This attitude undercuts our motivation to remain physically healthy. Unless this attitude is changed, physical deterioration takes place.

When our bodies are in poor condition, we diminish our ability to cope with emotional anguish. Less able to cope with emotional stress, we are tempted more than ever to stop living. Any reduction in our will to live only compounds our eating, sleeping, and exercise problems. And so, a destructive spiral is set in motion. This spiral can lead only to illness if it is allowed to continue.

### Grace

How does grace come to us in this situation? It comes in all the ways we are reminded about the gift of life and the responsibility of living. It comes through those people who encourage us to eat balanced meals and to be as physically active as we are able. It comes through all those persons, insights, and events that reveal to us we are in some way needed.

The temptation to quit can be strong. When we are ready to give up, we need to draw on resources outside ourselves. In such times it is necessary to turn to God and to others. When I have been especially low, I have found that I needed to turn to others as a way of seeking God's grace. In those low moments my prayers tend to be various ways of saying: "Poor me." When I reach out to others and express my feelings, I discover help. What I am unable to receive from God in private because of my emotional state, I discover I have a better chance of receiving through others.

In times like these we need to hear the Gospel proclaimed. The style of proclamation may or may not use traditional church language. But the message will proclaim the good news that we can have life, new life, even after experiences like Good Friday. There is hope—not only for the dying but also for those of us in grief.

Jesus said that there is comfort for those who mourn (Matt. 5:4). This comfort is the strength to face life as it is and the power to move on. Jesus pointed the way to strength for facing life and to power for moving on. He showed us that abundant life (life with an eternal quality to it) comes from our focusing on the will of God and on the needs of our neighbors. Jesus talked about the abundant life in terms of living a life of love. He warned us that to focus only on ourselves is destructive (Luke 9:24).

If we focus only on our grief (only on our sorrow and our loss), we are lost. But if we look beyond ourselves, there is hope. God's purpose for each of us is something more than not experiencing any heartache. God's purpose for

Jesus was certainly more than for Jesus always to be comfortable. Jesus was more important than that. So are we. We are made for loving. Our purpose in life has to do with all the implications contained in the commands to love God with our whole being and to love our neighbor as ourselves.

When we begin to recover our sense of purpose, the physical problems that may have accompanied our grief begin to disappear.

## ~7~

*To withdraw
from other people
is to withdraw from one
of the primary settings
God uses to give us
the grace we need.*

# Feeling So Alone

How can we endure the terrible loneliness that is part of our grief? How do we who have deeply enjoyed interdependence survive when a death thrusts us into the lonely position of independence?

## Three Lonely Individuals

### ~ Ellen ~

Ellen had enjoyed the bridge party. She was humming as she came into the bedroom, wondering what would be on television this late at night. She took off her necklace and was placing it in her jewelry box when she noticed a ring she had not worn in a long time.

He had given it to her on a vacation several years ago. A "just-because" gift, he had called it. From then on "just-because" was one of the ways they said, "I love you."

The feeling of loneliness hit her suddenly and hard. She could only stand there for a moment in silence with her eyes closed. All at once the room seemed as empty as outer space, and she felt its emptiness. She felt isolated and incomplete. Once again she was overwhelmed with the awareness that he was dead and she was alone.

It had taken only a moment for the warm after-glow of the bridge party to be smothered in the airless vacuum of her loneliness.

## ~ Eugene ~

Martha and Eugene had what they considered to be a good marriage. They had developed a team-work pattern of living over the years. Eugene did not realize how much he relied on Martha until she was dead.

It was not the functional dependence that surprised him. He knew there would be a big adjustment regarding keeping house, preparing food, and taking care of his clothes. He missed her friendship. He was surprised to discover how much he had come to rely on her friendship.

Eugene had not realized how vital she was to his decision making. Over the years he had developed the habit of talking with Martha about everything from major vocational decisions to less crucial decisions such as whether or not to buy a new sport coat.

He missed this most. Eugene missed having someone to talk with about the routine and special decisions in living. Since her death, choices—even simple choices—seemed to trigger the empty ache of loneliness.

## ~ Ruth ~

Ruth and her husband grew up in an era and in a culture that clearly defined what was "man's work" and what was "woman's work." Because they shared this common background and because they loved each other very much, they were happily married for fifty-one years.

Both Bill and Ruth assumed one of the ways a man showed he was a man was to "take care" of his wife; this included taking care of all the family's business matters. Therefore, it is not surprising that before Bill's death, Ruth had never dealt with insurance or bank statements. She had not dealt with mechanics or repairmen. The largest check she had ever written was for groceries.

When Bill died, Ruth felt very alone and in her loneliness she felt very vulnerable. Her common sense and her self-confidence told her that she could figure out how to do what needed to be done, but inwardly she longed for him to be there to "take care" of her. Her loneliness for his companionship was intensified by her dependence on him for so many practical matters of daily living.

### Loneliness and Our Basic Aloneness

The more we relied on the person who is dead, the more intense our feelings of loneliness are. The more lonely we feel, the more clearly we are able to see the aloneness of our human condition.

There is a sense in which we humans are very much alone. Each of us is a unique person. No one has ever been who we are. No one has ever seen or felt or thought exactly what we have seen, felt, and thought. No other human being can ever know our inmost self. Because each of us is so unique, so special, each of us is somewhat isolated. To some extent aloneness is a basic fact of life. As separate, unique individuals, we can never fully understand one another; we can never be totally sure we know what another person is feeling or thinking. No one can know precisely what we are experiencing in our grief. Grief is a "lonesome valley" and no one can walk it for us; we have to walk it for ourselves.

Our feelings of loneliness can be intense. They can tempt us to believe not only that no one knows exactly what we are experiencing but that no one cares. We see our friends in their daily activities and we say to ourselves: "They don't really care. If they really cared, they would show it more." From this position of self-pity our feelings of loneliness can grow into the basic view we have of ourselves. When this happens, we tend to stop reaching out to other people. We say: "Well, if they don't care any more than that, I'm not going to bother with them."

### Fellowship Is Real Also

The biggest danger in this type of self-pity is that we will withdraw from other people. It is dangerous to stop reaching out to others. If we isolate ourselves, the only dimension of life we are able to experience is the lonely dimension. Then we are cut off from fellowship, an aspect of reality that is fundamental and basic to our lives.

Each of us is an individual, but we have been created to live together. Each of us is unique, but each of us is also a social creature. We have been made for community, not solitary confinement. This is part of the wisdom in our Hebrew-Christian heritage: "Then the Lord God said, 'It is not good that the man should be alone; I will make him a helper fit for him' " (Gen. 2:18).

The reality of our dependence on one another is just as powerful as the counter reality of our basic aloneness or independence. We need to accept both our independence and our need for community in order to be whole. It is through community—through other people—that God sustains and nourishes us. To withdraw from other people is to withdraw from one of the primary settings God uses to give us the grace we need.

### Our Choice

We dare not allow the pain of our loneliness to tempt us into withdrawing from other people. We have a choice. Our choice is not whether we will be lonely. Rather, our choice is whether we are going to surrender to our loneliness and live in the self-imposed isolation of withdrawal, or whether we will pick up our cross of loneliness and move on.

The Greek word for cross literally means an upright stake or pole (according to *The Interpreter's Dictionary of the Bible*). The word can refer to the instrument of execution or it can refer to the kind of stake that holds an animal or a tent in place. To pick up our cross is usually understood to mean that we are to pick up the burdens we have to bear. Would it be too inaccurate to say that this phrase can also mean to pick up what is tying us down, to pick up the stake we are tied to and move on? "Pick up the loneliness that is tying you down and move on" is part of what the Gospel tells us.

We dare not surrender to our loneliness; yet it is very painful. It can cause us to feel so empty, so helpless, so isolated, so defeated that we fall into despair. Loneliness can cause us to feel that God has abandoned us. We want to cry out, "Why go on?" Although we see the kind gestures other people are making and perhaps we even see some of the ways we are needed, the pain of our loneliness seems to drain us of the desire to keep going.

### A Message from Our Heritage

In these moments the word from the Gospel we need to hear is a message that is difficult to communicate. It is difficult to communicate because it is both stark and simple. It is difficult to communicate because we want to be rescued from pain. The first part of the message is "Suffering is part of life."

Only an adolescent who glories in the tales of suffering heroes and only someone who has not yet experienced suffering can say these words with ease. Only persons who have become so bitter in living that they enjoy seeing others share their pain can find satisfaction in expressing these harsh words of reality.

Jesus knew that suffering is part of life. He endured more than physical anguish. He experienced terrible loneliness. He saw persons with whom he had invested so much, turn and run and leave him alone. The one who had first realized the significance of his mission (the one he named Peter) denied him. From the cross—so far as human eyes could see—it seemed Jesus' ministry was a failure. "My God, my God, why hast thou forsaken me?" he cried (Matt. 27:46). Jesus knew the pain of loneliness, and he experienced the harsh reality of the first part of the message: "Suffering is part of life."

The second part of the message is no easier to communicate. It is too familiar to those of us who are religious, and it is too mysterious for those of us who are secular. The second part of the message is "God was in Christ." God—the Source of all that is—chose to experience what we experience, to endure what we endure. The Word became a human being. The Creator of life experienced life. The Creator knows suffering firsthand and what it is to be alone and lonely. God in Christ has been through what we are going through.

The third part of the message is also difficult to communicate because it demands such a leap of faith. The message is "God who was in Christ will give us what we need." The One who seemed so far away when Jesus cried, "Why hast thou forsaken me?" was really there. The Sustainer was there enabling Jesus to endure even in the terrible loneliness of his crying out. God was there, and the result was victory over the crucifixion. Just as Jesus was not rescued from his cross, we need not expect to be rescued from ours. And just as Jesus was not defeated by his cross, we need not be defeated by ours. The One who gave Jesus what he needed in his ordeal will give us what we need in ours.

Suffering is part of life. There are some "lonesome valleys" that each of us must walk, and no one else can walk them for us. This is the way life is. God knows this. From firsthand experience, God knows this; God was in Christ. Therefore, we are not without hope. Jesus has walked where we walk, and the One who enabled him will enable us.

# ~8~

We are anxious
because we doubt ever being
able to fill the gap caused by
this death, and we doubt
our ability to deal
with all that lies ahead.

# Fears and Doubts

### Insecurity

The feeling of insecurity is sometimes part of the grief process. A person who has been important to us is dead; a significant relationship we relied on has ended. Not only do we feel lonely and see our basic aloneness (see chapter 7), but also we experience some form of fear. What we had in the past, we will not have in the future. Ways of living that were familiar and comfortable have been disrupted, and we realize it will never be the same again. This awareness of "the way things really are" creates in us insecurity, if not outright fear.

"I am afraid," June said. "It is a strange kind of fear. It is like being on top of a tall building and looking over the edge and realizing there is no guardrail. I know I am safe on the roof; yet there is no guardrail to keep me from falling over the edge.

"Daddy was my guardrail. I did not lean on him, but just knowing he was there if I needed him made me feel secure. Now that he is gone, I feel this strange kind of fear. At times I feel so vulnerable; I see that now there is no one to protect me from falling over the edge."

### Anxiety

Perhaps the kind of fear our grief causes is anxiety. Anxiety has been described as fear without a clear object.

When we are anxious, we are afraid, but we do not know exactly what we fear. Engulfed by our grief we look into our future and feel a strong uneasiness. We begin to realize that we are going to have to live without someone who has been very important to us. We are anxious because we doubt ever being able to fill the gap caused by this death, and we doubt our ability to deal with all that lies ahead.

Marie was an elderly woman who had never taken care of business matters. When her husband died, not only did she feel lonely, she was anxious also. Her outlook on what remained of her life filled her with dread and fear. The one who had taken care of her was dead and now everything was her responsibility.

Marie doubted she could do it. She was afraid she would make a fool of herself. She was afraid she would be made fun of for not knowing how to take care of her money. She was afraid someone would take advantage of her ignorance and cheat her out of what little she had. She was afraid of having to experience the humiliation of poverty. She was afraid of becoming just a Social Security number in an impersonal, public nursing home. She was afraid she would die neglected and alone. When she looked into the future, all of these fears welded together into one big nameless fear. Doubting her ability to cope with all this, she experienced painful anxiety.

Bill's anxieties, fears, and doubts were different from Marie's. In chapter 5 (page 53) Bill's situation was described. His wife died when she was only twenty-six, leaving him with a four-year-old girl. He worried about being able to provide the kind of guidance and affection his daughter needed. He doubted that he would have enough emotional energy for both the demands of his job and the personal needs of his daughter.

## *Fear of a Different Future*

There are a variety of ways a death can cause us to feel insecure, anxious, and fearful. Without the person who meant so much to us, the future can seem frightening. In grief we can be so overwhelmed by what we have lost; we feel terribly—even hopelessly—inadequate. What lies ahead is a life that is new and strange. Aware of our loss and the very different kind of living that is ahead, we doubt our abilities.

Fear of the future and doubts about our abilities are not the only expressions of fear and doubt that are sometimes part of our grief. The death of someone who is close to us can wake our anxieties and fears regarding death itself.

## *Fear of Death*

"What happened to Granddaddy?" the little girl asked.

"He died; he got so sick he could not get well," her mother answered.

"But what happened to him when he died?"

The little girl's question is our question when we face death. It is a factor in our fears. What happens? I had never really thought much about death until Dad died. I think for the first time in my life I was really aware that I too will die. It scared me. Death is an unknown. Unknowns can be frightening.

I remember a conversation I had while in college. Several of us were discussing what we thought happened after death. We talked about whether or not there is life after death. We rambled on about persons who were never "Christian" and yet who seemed to love God and their neighbor. What happened to them when they died? Is there a heaven and a hell? What about the "bad people" who did not know any better? It was a typical sophomore's religious "bull session." There was probably more noise than substance to it. Certainly more issues were raised than were settled.

Dr. Ennis Hill, who was then pastor of the First Methodist Church in San Angelo, Texas, quietly listened to our discussion. Finally someone asked, "What do you think, Dr. Hill?"

He said: "Do you believe God is the wisest of the wise and that God really is a God of love?"

"Well, yes," we replied.

"Then," Dr. Hill smiled, "why worry? Whatever is wisest and most loving is what will happen in death. We may not be able to say exactly what that is, but because God is wise and loving, we do not have to worry about it."

Dr. Hill's response leads us to the another discussion, faith in God. His statement is what I call the common sense of faith. It takes faith to be able to say what he said. Dr. Hill's profoundly simple response said in effect: "You say God can be trusted; well, trust God."

### The Common Sense of Faith

In dealing with the fears and doubts that come in our grief (such as those described in this chapter), the basic issue has to do with trusting God. Can we trust God to provide what we need in our new situation? Can we trust God to help us face our drastically altered lives? Can we trust God as we face our own deaths? Can God be trusted?

When we ask this question, we are not asking a question with our heads as much as we are asking a question with our hearts. Aching with grief and tangled in feelings of fear and doubt, we are not wanting academic, theological proof that God can be trusted. We yearn for a more personal assurance that speaks to our hearts. On another day when the experiences of grief are less intense, we will be ready for a more orderly and disciplined dealing with the theological issues that are involved. In our anguish we long for assurances more than for arguments. We long for witnesses more than for lectures.

Thus, we are impatient with persons who want to give us theology lessons in the midst of our grief. This may be so because we are intuitively aware that what we need is faith, and faith does not come at the end of an argument. How faith comes to us is a mystery. We seek it, and yet it always comes as a gift of grace.

### Some Ways Grace Comes

God's grace comes in many ways. For example, one of the ways in which God supplied courage to Ruth (refer to pages 72–73) was in her memory of what Aunt Louise had gone through. Ruth remembered that Aunt Louise was twenty-six when her husband died in 1904. She was left with three small sons, ages three, five, and eight. She was on a ranch that was ten miles from the nearest town, two miles from the nearest neighbor, and hundreds of miles from the nearest relative. Before she married, Louise had never lived on a ranch. There were none of the conveniences we take for granted, such as a telephone that could be used to call for help or a car to drive quickly into town for supplies or running water that made cooking and cleaning easier. Louise stayed on the ranch and somehow she survived until she learned enough about ranching to do more than merely survive. Although most people said she would fail, she did not. Her sons became respected men in the area, and her ranch made more than a comfortable living. Ruth remembered Aunt Louise, and she drew courage from those memories.

In our grief each of us can draw on our memories. We can remember other persons who have gone through ordeals similar to ours. We remember that they made it with the help of God, and we can trust that we will make it also. We can remember difficult times we have survived in the past. God was helping us then (whether we realized it or not), and God will not forget us now.

Another way God's grace can come to us is through the wisdom and promises found in our Hebrew-Christian heritage, especially in some of the Bible stories. Jesus Christ, our Redeemer, is the prime example of this promise. God did not allow the Crucifixion to remain a defeat, but transformed it into victory through the Resurrection. God kept the promise. The story of God's promise to Abraham is another example. Part of God's promise in Gen. 12:1-3 was that Abraham would be the father of a multitude, a great nation. But year after year Abraham and Sarah were childless. They became discouraged, gave up on God, and tried to take matters into their own hands. Their faithless actions led to the story of Ishmael (Gen. 16). But God kept reminding Abraham of the promise. Could God be trusted? That is clearly the implied question behind the ancient stories of Abraham.

Finally, when Abraham and Sarah were very old, messengers from God came to Abraham to tell him Sarah was going to give birth to a son. This story is so important, Genesis contains two versions of it. In one version (chapter 17) Abraham laughs at the news; in the other (chapter 18), Sarah laughs at God's promise. But the baby came. God kept the promise.

Just as God fulfilled the promise for Abraham and Sarah, God was faithful to the Israelites. God did not forget the Israelites in slavery in Egypt. God kept the promise. God did not abandon the people when they were in Babylon. God kept the promise.

Over and over the stories of the Bible remind us that God can be trusted. Our awareness of the wisdom and promises in these stories can be one of the ways God's grace comes to us when we are tangled in the doubts and fears of grief.

As we have observed before, people are the primary instruments God uses to give us the grace we need. God uses persons such as Aunt Louise and Abraham and Sarah. God uses the people who have kept the stories of Aunt Louise and Abraham alive for us. God also uses the neighbor who lives next door or the person who works with us or the one on our bowling team. It is persons such as these that God uses to meet our mundane and practical needs. The man who had never operated a washing machine until his wife died was helped by his next door neighbor. Marie's fear that she could not take care of business matters is the kind of fear God can heal through a neighbor's help and concern.

One of the major blocks to this expression of God's grace is our unwillingness to ask for help. Too often we are willing to ask God in secret for help while being unwilling to admit our need to a neighbor. Although this unwillingness to ask a friend to help is sometimes rationalized as "I don't want to be a bother," it is more often than not a form of pride. Our unwillingness to admit to a friend that we need him or her is usually a symptom of our unwillingness to be humble. What else is humility but the open admission of need? Our unwillingness to admit our need to friends makes our prayers to God hollow. We are saying: "God help me but do not allow anyone to see that I need anything." It is as if we asked God to help and then tied God's hands.

Our pride can block God's grace. Just as the Pharisees blocked their ability to receive the forgiveness that was available by refusing to admit their sin, we block our ability to receive the grace offered us in our grief by refusing to admit our needs. The grace is there; it is given. All we have to do is ask and receive it. (Read the parable and the comments that follow it in Luke 11:5-13.)

# ~9~

Our anger
cannot hurt God,
but our
pretended acceptance
and our phony faith
can hurt us.

# Anger
꙳꙳꙳&꙳꙳꙳

### Anger Toward the Dead

No one was in the cemetery except Sandra. She came to see if the gravestone had been delivered. It had not; there was only the little metal marker stating his name and the date of his birth and death. It was the lonely decoration on the grave; all the funeral flowers had dried and been thrown away. Sandra stood looking down at the bare dirt mound of her husband's grave.

*Why?* she inwardly shouted at him and at the universe. *Why did you die and leave me all alone?* There was anger in her tears. *Why did you leave me with so much unfinished? How dare you die with the business in such a mess and the kids only half grown . . . Am I going crazy? He did not want to die. He did not volunteer to have cancer . . . but I am angry! I wish you were here to . . . what is wrong with me? He loved me. I loved him . . . but it is so unfair. People say they are sorry you died. Well, I'm sorry I am alive. I wish all this were your problem now instead of mine. You could have made all this easier on me, but you didn't. You wasted precious time, and now I have to pay.*

Sandra's fists clinched. Her body was tense and shaking. Her eyes were red from the tears of sorrow and anger.

The aches and fears that are part of our grief can stimulate feelings of anger, even anger toward the person who died.

### Anger Toward God

Sometimes our grief expresses itself in anger toward God. This happens often in the grief that follows the death of a young person.

Paul was only nineteen when he died. He was bright with many talents, and it seemed he had a great future ahead of him. But Paul's sore leg had been more than an ache. It had been a symptom of a fatal form of bone cancer.

"I thought God was supposed to be a God of love," said one of his friends. "After what has happened to Paul, I do not see how anyone can recite that stuff about how much God loves us. How dare anyone tell me I am supposed to love God after God let this happen to Paul!"

### Anger Toward the Living

Not only can grief cause us to be angry toward the person who died and toward God, but also our grief can explode in anger toward friends or family members.

Carol was helping her mother clean out her father's closet and workroom. It was one of those necessary ordeals that follows the funeral. Carol sorted the items to discover what should be thrown away, what should be given away, and what should be kept.

"What do you mean, throwing away these papers?" Anger was in her mother's voice. "Your father worked hard on this material. How dare you throw it away! I thought you loved your father more than that."

"Mother, what good are these papers to us? We can't keep everything."

"These papers were important to your father; we just can't throw them away. It would be like throwing him away. It is bad enough for him to be dead, without you—his own flesh and blood—treating his work like garbage."

Anger is a powerful reality that can be set loose by a death. When someone we love dies, we are hurt. It is not unusual to feel that the timing of the death (if not the death itself) is unfair. On top of this, death sometimes thrusts problems and situations on us we would never choose for ourselves. When we have drawn a great deal of security and satisfaction from a relationship, we can feel robbed when the other person dies.

The angers in grief that have been illustrated thus far are: anger at the dead person, anger at God, and anger at another person. In each case, the person in grief felt threatened or victimized. These feelings triggered the anger.

### Grace in Anger

God's grace can be seen in our anger, especially when our anger is stimulating positive action. For example, anger might be the tool God uses to push Sandra into taking charge of her life in a new way.

*I'm not going to do to our kids what you did to me,* Sandra thought. *I will not leave with everything undone. I'll show you! I'll straighten this mess out yet.* Sandra walked away from the grave determined to take charge of her life.

Anger is one of the signals God has given us to alert us that something may be wrong. Carol's mother went to her bedroom after her harsh words with her daughter. "Why did I blowup like that? She is only trying to help." Introspection might reveal some fears that need to be faced, expose some unresolved guilt, or bring some conflicts she had with Carol to the surface. This revelation makes possible both resolution of the conflict and reconciliation in the relationship.

Anger can draw our attention to aspects of life we have ignored. Paul's friend may discover in his anger toward God that he has not thought much about what he believes.

In his angry struggle to relate his understanding of God's love to his view of human suffering, he may discover a more profound belief in God.

### Anger Can Be Destructive

Anger can be a helpful tool of God's grace. It can also be destructive because it is a powerful emotion. The greater the anger, the greater the power. When we lose control of our anger, it can hurt us and others.

Anger can become bitterness and resentment. This happens when we focus on the wrongs that have happened to us. When we dwell on our hurts and on the injustices that have happened to us, our attitude begins to decay. We stop living and growing. We are no longer in control of our anger; our anger controls us. "If only 'that' had not happened," we tell ourselves, "how much better our lives would be." We stop living, and we rot in the resentment that "he" or "she" or "it" ruined our life.

Resentment and bitterness are tempting because once we can blame "X" for our disappointments and unfulfilled dreams, we can live in the illusion that we are not responsible for our lives. We can pretend that we are free from accountability: "After what has happened to me, how else could I be?" But the price we have to pay for not being held responsible is living in bitterness and resentment.

If we focus on the wounds we have received, we lash out at others; we kick; we gripe; we tear down. When we hurt others, they tend to inflict some sort of pain on someone else. Like the spoiled apple in the barrel, we spread our decay. Anger can set in motion a destructive chain reaction.

Anger is a powerful reality. It can be a catalyst for positive action, but it can also be a very negative force in our lives.

### The Temptation to Deny Anger

Because it is so powerful and because it can be so destructive, some of us try to deny our anger. When we feel we have been wronged, we deny ourselves the right to feel angry. The result is that we usually feel depressed, and in our depression we are the object of our own anger.

If Sandra were to deny her anger toward her husband, the reality of those feelings would seek another object. She would probably feel anger toward herself, a form of depression or self-contempt: "If I had been a better wife, this might not have happened. If I were a better person, all this mess would not bother me. I hate myself for being so helpless."

If Paul's friend denied his anger toward God, his feelings of anger would seek another object. It might be the doctors or Paul's parents. But if he denied any expression of his anger, it would turn inward on himself. Perhaps it would take the form of feeling guilty because he lived while his friend died.

If Carol's mother tried to bottle her fears and anger inside herself, they would eat on her. It might take the form of depression and self-contempt. If the secret behind her anger is the fear that her life does not matter and that no one, not even her children, really care, then her bottled feelings would lead to painful despair.

Anger is a powerful reality. If we deny our anger, it usually turns inward and becomes a form of depression. We have to deal with it or it will deal us more misery.

### The Gospel and Anger

When our grief expresses itself in anger, what does the Gospel offer us? What are some of the expressions of God's grace that relate to the anger in our grief?

We can affirm that anger is a good gift. It is like the gift of a good broom. Of course, a broom can be misused. It can be used like a weapon to beat others over the head. However, the possibility of misuse does not change the fact that it is a good gift.

Earlier we noticed that anger can be a catalyst for positive change. The push anger gives us is sometimes the shove we need to begin working to make life better for ourselves and others. Sometimes it takes a burst of anger to set us doing what we should have been doing all along.

### Anger: a Gift for Relationships

Anger is a good gift to help us in our relationships with other persons. It is one of the brooms God has given us to sweep the harmful behavior out of our relationships. This is easiest to illustrate in a marriage; however, the basic insight is true of all relationships. Marriages seldom fall apart because of a single crisis. More often than not, they fall apart because of "the last straw." Often the correction of that "last straw" does not make the marriage any better. The reason is that the marriage wagon has been carrying too heavy a load of "straw" for too long. Anger can be seen as a gift God gives us to keep the "straw" from piling too high on the wagon.

It is helpful for Sandra to work through her anger toward her husband so that she can move beyond that anger. Buried in her mind are some good memories that could console her and give her strength. But she cannot get to those memories and feelings until she has swept the "straw" away. Anger can be a good broom.

### Anger and Our Relationship with God

The Gospel tells us that God is strong; our anger is not going to hurt God. There is much suffering in life that we cannot understand. The suffering of the innocent or the loss of a life before that person has reached his or her potential is a terrible mystery with which we have to live. It is not unusual for such tragedy to cause us to be angry with God.

Our anger cannot hurt God, but our pretended acceptance and our phony faith can hurt us. Our pretensions do not fool God and what is worse, they block us from a genuine relationship with God. How can God relate to us and deal with our hostility toward God if we play pretentious games? How can God deal with our doubts if we are pretending to have faith? When we consume our energies by pretending to love and have faith, we have no energies left to seek the message that God desires to give us.

When we are confronted by the terrible mysteries in life, we are placed in a situation similar to Jacob's (Gen. 32). In the midnight hours Jacob wrestled with an angel. If Jacob had walked away from that fight, refusing to wrestle with the angel of God because of some phony, pious excuses, he would not have received the blessing; he would not have become Israel. But Jacob wrestled and although he never walked the same again (his hip was thrown out of joint), he was blessed; he became Israel.

There are times when we are alone in the darkness of our living, and we have to wrestle with mysteries we cannot comprehend. In these grim ordeals of living, we must be open with God if we are going to be open to God. The blessing (whatever that is) will come only as we hang on as Jacob did and abandon neither our faith nor our integrity.

To be open to the blessing God would give us in our new situation, we must be open with God—even about our anger toward God. The Gospel assures us that God not only can take our anger but that in our honest struggles of faith, God reaches out to us.

### Anger Toward Others

What about the kind of anger Carol's mother expressed? What does the Gospel say to that? Her anger was probably an explosion of several fears she had bottled inside. They may have been fears of her ability to cope; they may have been fears that death will wipe away her labors; they may have been fears that if Carol did not see her father's papers as important, Carol might not see her mother's efforts worth much either. Her outburst of anger was probably the explosion of these or other unrecognized fears.

The only way to handle fears (as opposed to them handling us) is to face them and work through them. Our anger is one of the clues we have that points to what really scares us. Anger is often the first way our fears express themselves. Becoming aware of our anger can be the first step toward facing our fears.

In the conversation that might have flowed from the confrontation regarding the papers, Carol's mother might be set on the road to coping with her new situation. This is more likely to happen if Carol's mother is willing to explore why Carol's actions made her angry. The answer probably (although not necessarily) lies more with Carol's mother than it does in the actions of Carol.

### When Anger Is Misused

All of this says that anger is a good gift. But implied in this view of anger is the assumption that we will use this gift properly. What about our misuses of this gift? What about the times we have used this broom more like a weapon than a tool? What does the Gospel offer us who have misused the anger in our grief?

Through the Gospel we are given the reality of forgiveness. As was stated in chapter 5, forgiveness is something more than merely overlooking events in the past. The forgiveness a parent gives a child is rooted in the parent's awareness of the potential his or her love sees in the child. And when I, the child, sense my potential is more important than my past wrongs, I have a new lease on living. Forgiveness is the gift of a new view of the present and the future. To receive forgiveness is to obtain a new perspective on our lives. The past is not forgotten and the inevitable consequences of the past are not avoided. But here is a new view of what is important. Instead of being dominated by the awareness of the ways we have misused our lives in the past, we are free to focus on the positive possibilities that remain.

Forgiveness does not undo what we did, nor does it stop the consequences of our deeds. However, we see life in a new light. In this new light we accept that what is past is behind us. We no longer live in bondage to our misuse of the past. We may still be paying some of the consequences, but our focus, our attention, is not dominated by the old guilt but by new hope. In this new hope we sense positive possibilities in the present and in the future. We can even sense positive possibilities in the consequences of our wrong deeds. We have been given newness of life. We experience a kind of renewal.

In the awareness of this forgiveness for ourselves, we are able to forgive others. The past hurts they caused us may not be entirely forgotten. Certain scars may stay with us, but we now focus on new and positive possibilities both for ourselves and for them. This emphasis on new life buries the old. The new perspective we have on our lives spreads to all of our relationships. We who have received forgiveness, forgive.

# ~10~

There seems to be
an unwritten law in our society
that states that it is okay
to cry at the time of death and
at the time of the funeral,
but we should get all our emotional
stuff out of us within a few days.

# Hiding Our Grief

ᚠᚠᚠ❦ᚠᚠᚠ

"How are you getting along?" It was clear from the tone of the question that Mark was not just making polite conversation.

"Oh, I'm doing okay," Jack replied, not really answering the question. He knew Mark was genuinely concerned, but he was afraid to share his deep ache and sadness. Only three weeks had passed since the funeral of his daughter. Jack was afraid he would cry if he allowed himself to start talking about his grief. That might cause Mark to feel uncomfortable. It would be embarrassing and awkward.

Mark opened the door to allow Jack to share his grief, but Jack was afraid to go through that door. He hid his grief rather than risk crying. He hid his grief out of some fear that it might make his friend uncomfortable if he showed the depth of his sorrow.

### Some Reasons Why We Hide Our Grief

The farther we move from the time of the death, the more difficult it is for many of us to admit or express the sorrow in our grief. There seems to be an unwritten law in our society that states that it is okay to cry at the time of death and at the time of the funeral, but we should get all our emotional stuff out of us within a few days. Both we who shed the tears and those who are near us tend to feel shades of awkwardness and embarrassment.

This is a major reason why after the first few crisis days of the death and funeral, we tend to lock our grief inside ourselves. We do not want to impose on our friends or cause them to feel uncomfortable. We do not want to risk exposing our friends' inability to cope with our grief. So, we keep it to ourselves. We choose to grieve alone rather than risk making a friend feel awkward or inadequate.

"After all," we tell ourselves, "what could they do, anyway?"

Attitudes in our society encourage us to hide our grief. Since many people in our culture find it difficult to deal with the reality of death, we are tempted to hide our grief so that they will not be reminded of death. But once we begin to hide our grief from others, it is not long until we are trying to hide our grief from ourselves.

We are a "fix-it" culture that likes to do things quickly. We want fast, practical results. This attitude is a factor in our temptation to hide our grief. We are uncomfortable with grief that we cannot "fix" quickly. Our friends want to *do* something "to make it better" and there is very little they can do. This inability to "fix-it" tends to cause our friends to feel inadequate and awkward. When we sense what our grief is causing them to feel, we are embarrassed. Little wonder so many of us avoid facing grief in ourselves or in others.

### A Congenial Conspiracy

In our grief we often find ourselves caught in a cycle of behavior that is not helpful. We do not want our friends to feel inadequate; therefore, we do not talk about anything that might trigger our sorrow. Our friends pick up signals from us that we had rather not talk about it. So, they try to help us by not talking about anything they fear might cause us to feel sad. In their attempt to help us it is not unusual for our friends to give the dead person the silent treatment whenever we are around. It is as if our friends had never known the person who died. Yet, how helpful it would be for us to talk and cry and laugh together as we share our memories. But they are afraid of upsetting us, and we are afraid of causing them to feel awkward. Thus we join in a congenial conspiracy to deny our grief.

This unexpressed agreement between our friends and us not to stimulate or expose our grief, creates the illusion that our grief is ending only a short time after it began. In truth, the grief has merely gone underground.

In this period of publicly silent grief, some begin to think: "There must be something wrong with me; the funeral was weeks ago, and yet I am still grieving."

### No Timetable

Grief has no timetable anymore than grief has a set pattern for all people. Each grief experience is unique. One of the dangers in a book like this is that of creating the illusion that the process of grief is a fixed process. It is not. The grief each person experiences is a unique happening. This is certainly true regarding the length of time each person experiences intense feelings of sorrow.

These intense feelings come and go like waves washing over a beach. The waves are high and forceful. Then, there will be a period of relative calm before the waves of sorrow wash over us again. For some persons the waves come and go for a few days. For most persons this period of fairly frequent experiences of intense sorrow lasts several weeks. For others it is spread over a period of several months.

The time it takes to work through these waves of intense feelings is not important. What is important is that we work through them. What is important is that we not allow the uncomfortable feelings many people have in the presence of our sorrow to tempt us to deny or hide our grief.

### Grief Like a River

To try to deny our grief is like trying to stop a river from flowing. We may succeed in building a dam and not allowing any water down stream, but the water backs up and floods other ground. We may dam our grief's more natural expressions; however, the steady flow of its reality will cause it to flood into other areas of our living. Building a dam (denying our grief) does not stop the water from building up; it merely blocks the water from its natural course and makes it seek other outlets.

Bill tried to cut his grief short. His emotions found other outlets. He became quick-tempered. The slightest aggravation caused him to explode. He was hypercritical of everyone who worked with him. He blocked his grief but his temper overflowed.

### Part of Life

Grief is not something we need to hide as if it were something to be ashamed of. Grief is a part of life. The Bible reminds us that part of what it is to be fully human is to grieve. Grief stands at the crossroads of love and mortality. We humans can love; we humans are mortal; therefore, grief is inevitable. Grief happens when love has to deal with the limitations placed on life, especially the limitation of death. The only way we could avoid grief is to avoid caring and loving. But that is no choice at all. Our grief is the inevitable consequence of being mortal creatures who love.

*An Opportunity*

Yet, we can say more than that grief is an inevitable experience in life. We can find the motivation we need to face our grief when we realize it can be used as an opportunity for growth. Grief is certainly not the kind of opportunity we choose. It is a painful experience that is thrust upon us. But once we find ourselves in the anguish of grief, we can use this experience for growth. In fact, we either use the experience for growth or we suffer some sort of decay.

Who can say what types of growth a person can have in the midst of grief? Through their struggles with grief some people might discover new talents and opportunities. Other people might grow in their ability to accept love. Others might discover new depths in their lives and in their faith. Others might . . . who can say? (See chapter 11.)

It is not important to list all the ways grief can be used for growth. It is important to be aware that grief—never desired and always painful—can be used for good. We do not have to look on it as a burden to be hidden or denied. It is a burden, to be sure, but it can be a burden that has positive potential within it.

All of this is to say that God's grace can and does work through our grief. Therefore, it is neither appropriate nor helpful to us to try to deny or repress our grief. Our denials are only roadblocks in the way of God's grace.

*What About Our Friends?*

What about the uncomfortable feelings our friends seem to have? What shall we do? We shall love our friends enough to allow them to love us. An amazing thing about love is that when it is expressed in a mature way, it is a two-way reality: it helps the ones we love, and we also receive some benefits. We will love our friends enough to be honest with them. We will love our friends enough to give them the chance to be our friends. We will love our friends enough to let them know that we need them. Is there any bigger gift than the gift of being needed?

In our grief we need other people. To be sure, there is a dimension of our grief that only we can know and only we can endure in solitude. But a primary source of strength, one of the primary ways we are strengthened by God's grace, is through the love we receive from others.

When we are in grief, especially when we are in this silent period, we can call on our friends to be with us. How helpful it would have been to both Mark and Jack, if Jack could have reached out to Mark. Suppose Jack had expressed his grief openly:

"How are you getting along?" It was clear from the tone of the question that Mark was not just making polite conversation.

"Oh, in terms of surface routines, I guess I'm okay. But Mark, the ache is still there. (Tears come to his eyes.) There are times when I don't think I can make it."

"It must be rough. Is there *anything* I can do to help?" It is obvious that Mark is somewhat uneasy but it is also obvious that Mark really cares.

"Just having friends like you helps. It really does."

No problems were solved. There were no great breakthroughs into new, profound insights. It was simply an experience of intimacy, but it is through such experiences that we receive the grace we need to cope with our grief.

Anyone who has shared in such a simple and intimate experience is aware of the mystery that strengthens bonds of friendship. Jack loved Mark enough to share his grief. In the sharing of his grief he found new depth and strength in his friendship with Mark.

This can happen to us only if we refuse to hide our grief. God's grace can come to us through our friends' love and concern only if we do not play games.

# ~11~

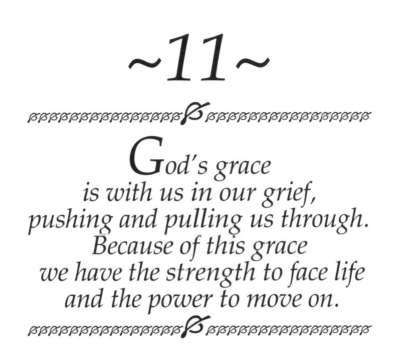

God's grace
is with us in our grief,
pushing and pulling us through.
Because of this grace
we have the strength to face life
and the power to move on.

# Beyond Grief . . . a New Life

God provides what we need from the moment we enter grief until slowly, gradually we discover that we have made it through the dark valley without being destroyed.

What is on the other side of grief? Beyond grief we discover new life. Just as each experience of grief is unique, the new life each of us discovers is different.

### *Two Illustrations*

#### ~ Mrs. Roberts ~

Mrs. Roberts loved her husband. They had been married more than forty years when he died. During their marriage they had developed a comfortable and creative relationship. This is not to imply they did not have their problems; however, she found meaning and contentment in helping her husband with his work. Both he and she understood his vocation to be "their" work. She depended on him and he depended on her. In public she felt comfortable allowing him to be "in the spotlight." An outside observer would have described her work as "woman's work."

When Mr. Roberts died, she felt as if the world had collapsed. Her grief was painful and long. She had never lived alone. The doubts and fears that come with grief made her tremble. But she moved on. She moved into a new life. She lived one day at a time until she had enough confidence to begin to face the future. She began to do the work her husband had done. She became involved in some activities that she never would have had the time or the desire to do if Mr. Roberts were alive. She was so effective in her labors that she received some recognition. Her friends saw her in a new light, and she began to have a new view of herself.

To this day, Mrs. Roberts wishes her husband were alive, growing old with her. But that is not a choice. The only choice Mrs. Roberts has is to move on to a new life or to decay by trying to hang on to yesterday. Mrs. Roberts chose life.

She has worked through the grief process. This is not to say that she is no longer touched by moments of sadness. One time she was visiting her son. He took her through the place where he worked, showing her what he had accomplished. She was proud. She longed for Mr. Roberts to be there to share this moment with her. Tears came to her eyes. When we have loved deeply and for a long time, that love stays with us. Because it was *love*, from time to time we are painfully aware of what we have lost.

### ~ Ron and Julie ~

Linda was only a child when she died. Her parents, Ron and Julie, could not believe she was dead. For years they had fought her disease. They had been told what to expect, but when it finally happened, they were surprised. They could not imagine life without Linda.

Their grief was lengthy. Their anguish, extreme. They had an especially difficult struggle with their anger. "Why would God allow this to happen?" Bitterness and resentment threatened to take over their lives.

Finally, they began to emerge from their grief. Ron and Julie continue to miss Linda. Even now that they are through the grief process, there are moments of intense sorrow. Although they have conquered the temptation to become bitter, they do not like what has happened. They wish she were alive and healthy. But they have faced reality. She is dead. Their choice has been the same as Mrs. Roberts'. They could face a new life without Linda, or they could dwell on the past and decay. They chose life.

From their ordeal they gained a new view of life. They saw how precious and fragile life is. They saw how big a gift it is. They discovered that the basic question is not "why is there tragedy?" The basic question is "why is life so good that tragedy is a possibility?" In the pain of their grief over what they had lost, they were able to celebrate the gifts they had been given.

### The Purpose of This Book

The purpose of this book has been to point to a truth about life. That truth is that God's grace is with us in all situations, even grief. Because of God's grace we can say YES to life, even when life is not the way we want it.

In chapter 1 we looked at Psalm 23:4: "Even though I walk through the valley of the shadow of death, I fear no evil; for thou art with me; thy rod and thy staff, they comfort me." Throughout this book we have observed that God's grace is with us in our grief, pushing and pulling us through. Because of this grace we have the strength to face life and the power to move on.

There is another verse from this psalm that is appropriate for us to consider in relation to grief: "Thou preparest a table before me in the presence of my enemies; thou anointest my head with oil, my cup overflows (23:5)." Life has a way of sitting us down in the presence of enemies. We do not choose grief and yet grief comes. It sits at our table of life like an enemy that would destroy us.

It is well to notice that we are "at a table." It is a place where we can be fed. God feeds us in the presence of the very enemies that would destroy us. We are placed in a situation we did not choose, and it is a dangerous situation. However, we need not be destroyed; there is food here. Not only can we be fed, we can be blessed. "Thou anointest my head with oil, my cup overflows." We are given more than we need to survive. We are given more than life; we are given life with an eternal quality, an abundant life.

Mrs. Roberts and Ron and Julie did not choose their sorrow. But, they were not destroyed. They were fed, even in their grief. Not only did they survive, they grew.

What is on the other side of our grief? Life! New life!

# The Twenty-third Psalm
ßßß*ß*ßßß

*The Lord is my shepherd, I*
*shall not want;*
*he makes me lie down in green*
*pastures.*
*He leads me beside still waters;*
*he restores my soul.*
*He leads me in paths of righteous-*
*ness*
*for his name's sake.*

*Even though I walk through the val-*
*ley of the shadow of death,*
*I fear no evil;*
*for thou art with me;*
*thy rod and thy staff,*
*they comfort me.*

*Thou preparest a table before me*
*in the presence of my enemies;*
*thou anointest my head with oil,*
*my cup overflows.*
*Surely goodness and mercy shall*
*follow me*
*all the days of my life;*
*and I shall dwell in the house of*
*the Lord*
*for ever.*

## ABOUT THE AUTHOR

The Reverend James L. Mayfield is a United Methodist pastor and has served Tarrytown Church in Austin, Texas since 1988. Prior to that he was Superintendent of the Austin District of the United Methodist Church.

The author is a native of Texas and has pastored churches throughout this state since 1963. Reverend Mayfield has also served as chairperson on various Annual Conference boards and agencies. He holds degrees from the University of Texas (Bachelor of Arts); Southern Methodist University, Perkins School of Theology (Bachelor of Divinity); Texas Christian University, Brite Divinity School (Doctor of Ministry); and Huston-Tillotson College (honorary Doctorate of Divinity).

Reverend Mayfield enjoys wood carving, fishing, and writing poetry. He has privately published five volumes of poetry. He is married to Rita Browning, and they have two children.